I Know Someone with Dyslexia

Sue Barraclough

www.raintreepublishers.co.uk
Visit our website to find out more information about Raintree books.

To order:
☎ Phone 0845 6044371
🖶 Fax +44 (0) 1865 312263
💻 Email myorders@raintreepublishers.co.uk

Customers from outside the UK please telephone +44 1865 312262

Raintree is an imprint of Capstone Global Library Limited, a company incorporated in England and Wales having its registered office at 7 Pilgrim Street, London, EC4V 6LB – Registered company number: 6695582

Edited by Rebecca Rissman, Daniel Nunn and Siân Smith
Designed by Joanna Hinton Malivoire
Picture research by Mica Brancic
Originated by Capstone Global Library
Printed and bound in China by Leo Paper Products Ltd

ISBN 978 1 406 22078 0
15 14 13 12 11
10 9 8 7 6 5 4 3 2 1

British Library Cataloguing in Publication Data
Barraclough, Sue.
I know someone with dyslexia. – (Understanding health issues)
1. Dyslexia–Juvenile literature.
I. Title II. Series
616.8'553-dc22

Acknowledgements
We would like to thank the following for permission to reproduce photographs: Alamy p. 26 (© Ben Molyneux), Capstone Global Library Ltd p. 16 (Richard Hutchings); Corbis pp. 23 (© cultura), 27 top (epa/© Jonathan Brady), 27 bottom (Retna Ltd./Rob Kim/© RD); Getty Images pp. 4 (Photodisc/Yellow Dog Productions), 14 (The Image Bank/Mark Scott); Photolibrary pp. 5 (Blend Images RM/Jose Luis Pelaez Inc), 6 (imagebroker.net/Norbert Michalke), 8 (imagebroker.net/Ulrich Niehoff), 9 (age fotostock/Javier Larrea), 10 (F1 Online/Paul Paul), 11 (Stock4B RF), 13 (Robert Harding Travel/Robert Harding Productions), 20 (age fotostock/Juan Manuel Silva), 24 (age fotostock/Beverly Logan), 25 (81A Productions), 27 middle (Tim Rooke); Science Photo Library p. 17 (Sheila Terry); Shutterstock pp. 15 (Laurence Gough), 18 (Pavzyuk Svitlana), 19 (Rob Marmion), 21 (Alexander V Evstafyev), 22 (Monkey Business Images).

Cover photograph of a girl reading a magazine reproduced with permission of Corbis (Blend Images/© Jose Luis Pelaez, Inc.).

We would like to thank Matthew Siegel, Ashley Wolinski, and Bernadette McLean for their invaluable help in the preparation of this book.

Contents

Do you know someone with dyslexia?. 4

What is dyslexia?. 6

Understanding dyslexia 10

What causes dyslexia? 12

Living with dyslexia 14

Things that can help. 16

How does it feel?. 20

Being a good friend 22

How can I help? 24

Famous people with dyslexia. 26

Dyslexia - true or false? 28

Glossary. 30

Find out more 31

Index 32

Some words are printed in bold, **like this**. You can find out what they mean in the glossary.

Do you know someone with dyslexia?

Someone with dyslexia may be clever but can have problems with reading or writing. A person with dyslexia may avoid reading in class but may love talking and telling stories.

Some people with dyslexia can find it hard to read or write.

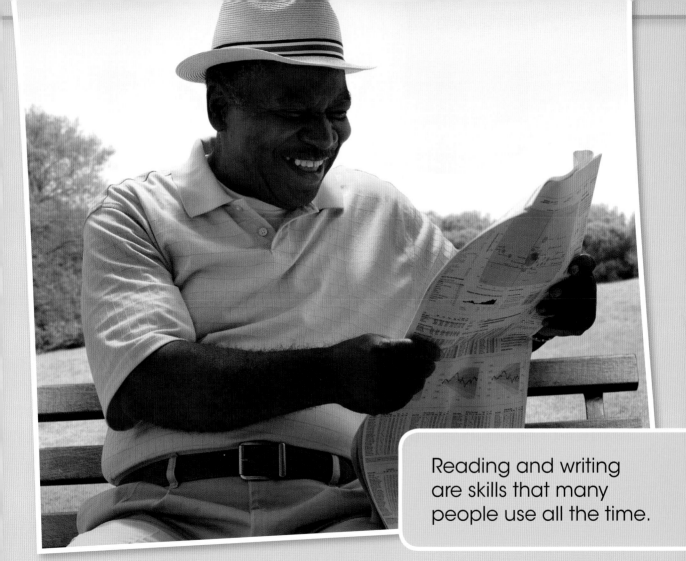

Reading and writing are skills that many people use all the time.

Some people with dyslexia may find it hard to **concentrate** in class. Sometimes they do not understand what the teacher is saying.

What is dyslexia?

Dyslexia is something that affects the way a person thinks and learns. People who have dyslexia can have difficulties with reading, writing, or spelling.

Someone with dyslexia may find they have to work harder at reading, writing, or spelling than other people.

Dyslexia can mean:

- getting letters the wrong way round, such as reading or writing 'd' for 'b'
- seeing words as blurry, jumbled, or wrongly spaced
- seeing words as squashed together or even moving around
- not seeing numbers or letters in the correct order
- muddling letters, for example reading 'was' as 'saw'
- swapping letters, such as reading 'magazine' as 'mazagine'.

Someone with dyslexia may find it hard to tell the time or remember phone numbers.

Dyslexia can affect people in other ways, too. A person with dyslexia may find it hard to learn left from right. Someone with dyslexia may struggle to remember the order of things, such as the days of the week or months of the year.

Many people with dyslexia find that they also have different strengths. Some people with dyslexia are very **creative**, or imaginative, or good at solving problems in new ways.

People with dyslexia can sometimes be very good at music or art.

Understanding dyslexia

Learning to read and write is difficult to do. The brain needs to sort and store large amounts of information about letter shapes and sounds. Someone with dyslexia may find it very hard to understand how letters and words work.

Someone with dyslexia may find it hard to **sound out** words.

A person with dyslexia may find it easier to learn letters if they can touch them and feel their shape.

Many people with dyslexia say that they think in pictures rather than words. This means they can find it hard to understand words that they cannot link to a picture.

What causes dyslexia?

No one knows for sure what causes dyslexia. Scientists have found that some parts of the brain that are used for language work in a different way for a person who has dyslexia.

touch

movement

sight

speech

behaviour and feelings

hearing

Different parts of our brains control different things.

Some scientists think that dyslexia might be partly **genetic**. This means that it can run in families. So if a parent has dyslexia there is more chance that their child will have it too.

Some parents only realize that they have dyslexia when their children are tested.

Living with dyslexia

Dyslexia is part of who a person is. It does not go away as a person gets older. However, people with dyslexia can find different ways to use their strengths, and to manage their difficulties.

Children with dyslexia can grow up to become very successful adults.

It is important to talk about problems with reading or writing as early as possible. It is more likely that you will get extra support in school and this will help with tests and exams later.

Someone with dyslexia might be given extra time to finish an exam.

Things that can help

A person with dyslexia may need to find different ways to read and write, or to learn and remember. There are lots of different things that can help with this. Each person needs to find out what works best for them.

It can be easier to read words written on the board if you sit near the front of the classroom.

Some people with dyslexia wear **tinted** glasses to help them read.

Some people with dyslexia find it easier to read words on a coloured background. Using different coloured glasses or printing words on different coloured paper can help with this.

Using computers often helps people with dyslexia. Some computers can be set up to recognize speech, so a person with dyslexia can record thoughts and ideas without having to spell or write.

Words come up on this computer screen when they are spoken into the microphone.

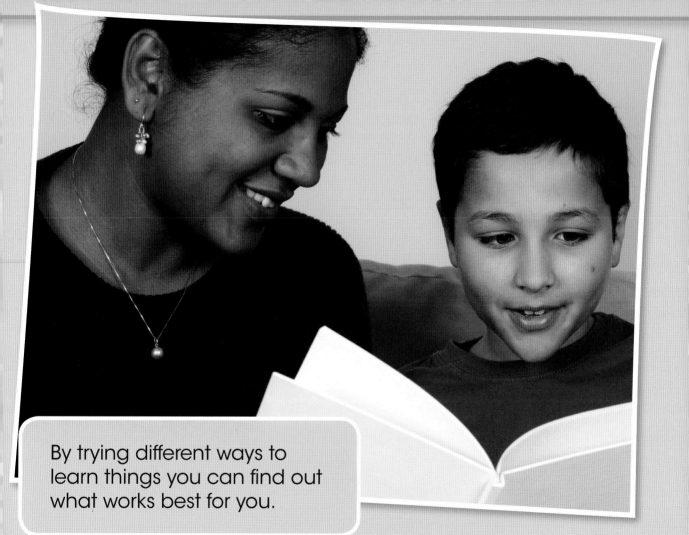

By trying different ways to learn things you can find out what works best for you.

Many people with dyslexia find that having extra help in the classroom can be useful. This may be a one-to-one session with the teacher or helper, or working with a small group.

How does it feel?

Someone with dyslexia may feel angry or sad that they cannot do certain things well. They might feel **frustrated** that it takes them longer to do things that other people can do quickly.

Someone with dyslexia might feel annoyed if they keep confusing their left shoe and their right shoe.

This man is an artist. Being able to think of new ideas is a useful skill for many jobs.

But people with dyslexia often find that they are good at things that other people find hard. They can often be good at coming up with ideas and finding ways around problems.

Being a good friend

You can be a good friend to someone with dyslexia by understanding that they have a difficulty with words. Someone with dyslexia may have problems understanding what is said.

Be patient. If a friend does not understand something, say it again in a different way.

A good friend likes us for who we are.

A good friend values the things we do well. If someone says something unkind or untrue about a person with dyslexia, try to explain why they are wrong.

How can I help?

Some people with dyslexia find it hard to find the right words when speaking. If someone with dyslexia feels hurried, they may become more muddled. Understand that someone with dyslexia may take longer to answer a question.

A friend understands that someone with dyslexia may know the answer but struggles to say the word.

The more you understand the more you can do to help.

Dyslexia can run in families so parents or older brothers and sisters can help younger children to learn. A parent or brother or sister with dyslexia can be very helpful because they understand the problem.

Famous people with dyslexia

Roald Dahl was a world famous writer who had dyslexia. His story, *The Vicar of Nibbleswicke*, is about a vicar with a made-up type of dyslexia. The book was used to raise money for dyslexia **research**.

Many of Roald Dahl's books have been made into films, such as *Charlie and the Chocolate Factory*.

Many famous people alive today have dyslexia. Others from the past may have had dyslexia, too. Some of these people are shown in the list below.

- Tom Cruise
- Walt Disney
- Leonardo Da Vinci
- Albert Einstein
- Keira Knightley
- Jamie Oliver
- Winston Churchill
- Whoopi Goldberg
- Richard Branson

Dyslexia – true or false?

Someone with dyslexia is more likely to be left-handed than someone without dyslexia.

TRUE! However, being left-handed does not mean that you have dyslexia.

There is no such thing as dyslexia. People who cannot read just aren't trying.

FALSE! People with dyslexia are often very bright. They often try very hard but because their brains work differently they may struggle to learn to read.

Dyslexia is very **rare** and only affects a small number of people.

FALSE! In fact, around one in every 10 or 20 people has dyslexia.

People grow out of dyslexia.

FALSE! Dyslexia is a part of who a person is and it does not go away as they get older. But people with dyslexia can find ways to use their strengths well and cope with any difficulties.

Glossary

concentrate give all your attention to something

creative having the talent and imagination to make new things. This might include a talent for creating art, music, or stories.

frustrated feeling annoyed because you cannot do something, or cannot do it well

genetic something that runs in families and is passed down from parent to child, such as having brown hair or green eyes

rare not happening or occurring very often

research investigate something to find out more information about it

sound out to read a word by saying the sounds the letters make and then putting these sounds together

tinted slightly coloured

find out more

Books to read

Dyslexia (Talking it Through), Althea
  (Happy Cat Books, 2003)

My Name is Brian Brain, Jeanne Betancourt
  (Scholastic, 1996)

Tom's Special Talent, Kate Gaynor
  (Special Stories Publishing, 2009)

Websites

kidshealth.org/kid
Visit Kids Health and type 'Dyslexia' in the
'Search here' box to learn more.

www.arkellcentre.org.uk
The Helen Arkell centre is the oldest dyslexia
centre in the country. Click on 'An A-Z' for a list
of famous people with dyslexia.

www.dyslexiacentre.co.uk
Click on the pictures to find out more about
dyslexia and explore useful links.

Index

brain 10, 12, 28

causes of dyslexia 12–13
coloured paper 17
computers 18
concentration 5
creative people 9, 21

Dahl, Roald 26–27

exams and tests 15

family members with dyslexia
    13, 25
famous people with dyslexia
    26–27
feelings 20
friends 22–23, 24
frustration 20

genetics 13
glasses 17

helping people with dyslexia
    24, 25

left and right 8, 20, 28
living with dyslexia 14–19

muddling and swapping
    letters 7

number of people with
    dyslexia 29

order of things 8

phone numbers 8

reading 4, 5, 6, 7, 10, 16, 17,
    28

school, extra help in 15, 19
sounding out words 10
spelling 6, 7
strengths 9, 14, 21, 29

telling the time 8
thinking in pictures 11

what dyslexia is 6–7
writing 4, 5, 6, 7, 10, 16